Incomparable
JAPANESE
GARDENS

© 2008 Gorazd Vilhar and Charlotte Anderson

Photographs by Gorazd Vilhar
Text by Charlotte Anderson
Produced by I&I Inc.
Art direction by Fumio Munakata
Book design by Hiroyasu Murofushi
Calligraphy by Jippo Ito
Photographs edited by Charlotte Anderson

Published by IBC Publishing, Inc.
Ryoshu Kagurazaka Bldg. 9F, 29-3 Nakazato-cho
Shinjuku-ku, Tokyo 162-0804, Japan
www.ibcpub.co.jp

First Edition 2008

ISBN978-4-89684-691-1

Printed in Japan

Incomparable
JAPANESE
GARDENS

日本の庭：比類なき美の世界

2008 年 5 月 12 日　第 1 刷発行
著　者　　ゴラーズ・ヴィルハー
　　　　　シャルロッテ・アンダーソン
発行者　　浦　晋亮
発行所　　IBC パブリッシング株式会社
　　　　　〒 162-0804 東京都新宿区中里町 29 番 3 号 菱秀神楽坂ビル 9F
　　　　　Tel. 03-3513-4511　Fax. 03-3513-4512
　　　　　www.ibcpub.co.jp
デザイン　室伏宏保（アイアンドアイ）
題　字　　伊藤十峰
印刷所　　大日本印刷株式会社

© Gorazd Vilhar and Charlotte Anderson 2008
© IBC Publishing, Inc. 2008

Printed in Japan
ISBN 978-4-89684-691-1

Incomparable

JAPANESE
GARDENS

Gorazd Vilhar and Charlotte Anderson

I B C
PUBLISHING

Contents

Introduction

Japanese garden arts remain unsurpassed in all the world. The antecedent of the garden in Japan was the primeval place of animistic worship—a simple clearing in a grove of trees. A paving of white pebbles and enclosure within straw ropes later began to formalize such spaces and mark them as sacred. Even in the distant mists of time, magnificent trees, boulders, and waterfalls had been viewed by the early Japanese as dwelling places of the divine, and they were similarly encircled by straw ropes, as they are today. One can imagine that such sensitivity to their natural environment would predispose them to the influence of the Chinese gardens described by the early court emissaries who returned from the continent with amazing reports of a highly developed civilization. Already in the Nara period (710–94), evidenced by archeological findings as well as the body of poetry passed down from that time, gardens imitating real and mythical natural vistas in the style of T'ang Dynasty gardens existed in Nara. And so it is that the Japanese have been involved in the art of gardening already for some thirteen centuries.

It is not surprising that Kyoto—the imperial capital for more than a thousand years, and the longtime center of Buddhism—is where the garden arts developed to their greatest heights. From the time the capital was moved there from Nara in the late eighth century, gardens became ever more splendid and gradually more Japanese. Masterly garden design arose as one of the highly regarded talents among the aristocracy of the Heian period (794–1185), and men of position and means surrounded their new villas with elaborate gardens. Only a few small fragments of such gardens remain, notably Shinsen-en, the imperial "Divine Spring Garden." Fallen to ruin and restored twice, today that garden is only about one-tenth its original size. Fortunately, much information has been gleaned from preserved scroll paintings, literature, and records, yielding an engaging, if incomplete, portrait of gardens of the day.

Nearly a thousand years ago, a Kyoto nobleman put brush to paper to set down the body of knowledge he had acquired about gardens in his lifetime. The resulting two scrolls of text, known as the *Sakuteiki,* comprise the oldest known treatise on the aesthetic art of gardening, not only in Japan but in the world. Although authorship of this ancient unsigned work has been debated through the centuries, current scholarship has settled on Tachibana-no-Toshitsuna, an eleventh-century courtier. As the son of Fujiwara-no-Yorimichi, a powerful imperial regent, he would certainly have been at home in the magnificent gardens of the capital.

In the Heian period gardening was a gentleman's art, and the Heian nobility vied to display perfection and refinement in the gardens surrounding their estates. It was partly by such cultural pursuits and skills that they would have been judged by their peers and, in that particularly romantic era, by potential lovers too. *The Tale of Genji,* celebrated as the world's first novel and document of that time, enchantingly describes a resplendent, courtly world of leisure, where amusement was the order of the day, and where time was given over to the pursuits of witticism, poetry, beauty, and love.

The *Sakuteiki* recommends looking to nature's most beautiful landscapes for inspiration, yet it advises that a garden should *reflect* nature, not copy it. Certainly, in those days, a part of garden appreciation stemmed from the viewer recognizing allusions to beloved spots of natural beauty in the wild surroundings of the city, far-flung sights they may have heard about from travelers or read about in poems, or ideals of Paradise in Buddhist scriptures.

In Heian-kyo, as Kyoto was then known, aristocratic *shinden-zukuri* palace-style mansions were attractively oriented to garden views from their verandas, as well as from outer rooms by way of moveable shutters or reed blinds. With the Japanese preference for plain and simple interiors, it seems that nearly all existing "decoration"

lay beyond in the impressive gardens, featuring streams, bridges and waterfalls, ponds and islands, with trees and other plantings and, of course, stones. Stones were crucial in Heian gardens, carrying with them the weight of historical Chinese garden wisdom, Buddhist philosophy, and Japan's own indigenous belief that certain extraordinary stones are earthly seats of the gods. The *Sakuteiki* counsels the proper setting of stones—a troubling art, it seems, for the author listed many taboos of the day: "If so much as one of these taboos is violated, the master of the household will fall ill and eventually die, and his land will fall into desolation and become the abode of devils."

The handling of water in gardens required special attention too, for certain directions were geomantically inauspicious. Water should not be made to flow toward the northwest, it was believed, or the fortune within the home would flow out with it. To the contrary, "the flow of water should come from the east, pass beneath the buildings, turn to the southwest, and thus wash away all manner of evil." Techniques for creating numerous styles and moods of islands, such as the ethereal "mist type" or the rugged "cove beach type" are offered. Precise instructions are given for the use of stones to captivating effect in the creation of streams and waterfalls. "It has been said there are many ways to make a waterfall, but no matter what, they should always face the moon," the ancient *Sakuteiki* advises, "so that the falling water will reflect the moonlight."

In time Buddhism, thanks to its greatly expanding popularity and its imperial and aristocratic patrons, accumulated great power and wealth. With their substantial means, temples commissioned fine works of sacred art— sculptures, scrolls, and paintings. Wondrous gardens were also created on temple grounds. These cultivated spots stood in contrast to the areas of abundant and untamed nature that then surrounded them. Rare rocks and careful plantings created beautiful scenes, infused with several layers of meaning. Some gardens emphasized changing landscapes as a viewer moved along a designated path. Others were meant to be seen through the enhancing frame of a window or open doors. Frequently created by the priests and monks themselves, many of the gardens sought to present a glimpse of Paradise on earth. As certain gardens came into their own in one or another of the seasons, they inspired feelings of pleasant anticipation, just as they do now.

Saiho-ji temple is affectionately known as Koke-dera, the "Moss Temple," for the more than one hundred varieties of moss that have come to carpet the ground, stones, and gnarled tree roots over the centuries. The garden's impressive naturalism misleadingly suggests not a garden but rather a magical corner of nature, undesigned, just discovered. Of course, therein lies the genius of this garden, reconstructed in the fourteenth century on the site of twelfth-century and even earlier gardens. In its cool depths, all is lush green, even the light, as it filters through the leafy canopy overhead and dapples the shaded water of a pond styled in the shape of the Chinese character for "heart." On the hillside, in the upper garden, an exceptional stone grouping is thought to be the predecessor of the dry landscape gardens that would become integral to the search for enlightenment at later Zen temples.

For all the restraint usually apparent in Japanese Buddhist architecture, the brilliant golden visage of the water pavilion at Kinkaku-ji tends to surprise. Built as a villa by the third Ashikaga shogun, Yoshimitsu, when he went into semiretirement at the end of the fourteenth century, after turning over his ceremonial duties to his nine-year-old son, apparently only its upper-story ceiling was originally gilded. Having already stood for five-and-a-half centuries, the "Golden Pavilion" was destroyed by an unfortunate fire in 1950. It was only then, in the reconstruction, that the façade was given its current appearance.

The pavilion is truly beautiful, set out over the "Mirror Pond" that has always been the centerpiece of this garden. It stands against the distant mountains and the verdant northern hills, one of which Yoshimitsu is said to have had draped with lengths of white silk on hot summer days to suggest a snowcap. He created the pond and its ten islets to be viewed from the pavilion and from the water itself, impossible today for any but the most extremely eminent of guests. Boating parties on garden lakes and ponds were a popular amusement of the day, in fact had been for centuries. And so it was that certain striking rock arrangements came to be tucked away on the far side of islets where they would only be revealed to boaters and might even serve as inspiration for their party poetry compositions. Not long after the retired shogun hosted his greatest garden party of all—a twenty-day extravaganza for the reigning emperor—he passed away, and in accordance with his wishes his estate became the Buddhist memorial temple that it remains today.

It was Yoshimitsu's grandson Yoshimasa, a child shogun like his own father, who created Ginkaku-ji in Kyoto's eastern hills. With limitless power concentrated in his hands, he was able to confiscate the ideal natural site from its owner, but many years would pass, due to war and unrest in Kyoto, before he could create the estate and garden of his dreams. When the time came, however, in the face of inadequate funds for such a grand project as he had imagined, he pressed for donations of workmen and materials from all the noble families. A diary of the day tells of one Lord Asakura sending three thousand of his men to transport trees from an old Ashikaga family palace ruin to help fill out the shogun's new garden. Other trees and stones were brought from far afield, taken from the wilds as well as pulled from existing gardens by shogunal order. A stroll garden was created at the foot of the forested hills, with the "Brocade Mirror Pond" reflecting the ornate patterns of the surrounding flora.

Yoshimasa was certainly inspired by the "Golden Pavilion"

and recreated a similar form here on a smaller scale, but his so-called "Silver Pavilion" was never leafed. Perhaps "silver" only suggested the moon, so deeply appreciated by cultured aesthetes. It is sure that he often sat at the window of his pavilion watching the moon rise over his garden, and it is likely that by moonlight he penned his famous poem which begins, "My lodge is at the foot of the 'Moon Waiting Hill'. . . ." With his eventual passing, his estate also was turned into a temple, and the pavilion is now its "Kannon Hall," where the goddess of mercy is enshrined. Near the pavilion is a later garden feature, an abstract "Sea of Silver Sand," while a flat-topped cone of sand reminiscent of Mt. Fuji stands on its "shore." Certainly one can imagine the shimmer the moon casts across that sand sea, and feel regret that the temple gates close to the public before sunset.

In the Kamakura period (1185–1333), when luxury and decadence gave way to martial values, the austere and disciplined Zen sect of Buddhism began to influence even the garden arts, leading to the golden age of gardens in the Muromachi period (1333–1573). In what was the second wave of Japanese–Chinese relations, disciples returning from study with Chinese Zen masters sought to emulate esteemed Sung-period ink landscape paintings of craggy mountains, rocks, trees, and waterfalls. These monochromatic paintings even inspired the creation of unique gardens poetically known as *kare sansui,* "mountains and waters without water." Through sand, pebbles, and rocks, a whole world of spiritual thought was represented, creating ideal places for meditative contemplation.

Kyoto possesses the greatest share of these dry landscape gardens—some consisting of no more than sand or gravel raked into simple, yet exquisite, patterns symbolizing elements of nature and Buddhist philosophy, while others bring rocks and sometimes moss or clipped shrubbery into the spiritual and artistic composition. The subtemple Daisen-in, within the vast Daitoku-ji monastery complex, is surrounded by such gardens, and is a feast for the eyes and spirit. Its East Garden depicts a masterpiece of landscape in miniature, with symbolic mountains, ravines, and a waterfall, all of stone. Each stone or stone grouping—"Crane Islet," "Treasure Mountain," "Stone of Experience," "Goddess of Mercy's Stone," "Buddha's Footprint," "White Cloud," "Tiger's Head"—is imbued with its own allegorical meaning, and together they speak symbolically of the complexity of human existence. A river of raked gravel issuing from the mountains divides into two, with one part flowing into the "Middle Sea" garden area, and the other into the greater "Ocean" stretching along the south side of the temple. From the ocean waves, represented by undulating lines, two small sand cones rise up to provide focal points for meditation.

Ryogen-in, another subtemple within the same monastic complex, boasts five gardens adjoining its *hojo,* or abbott's quarters. One of them, named A-Un, represents the truth of the universe and the inseparability of certain universal counterparts: heaven and earth, positive and negative, and inhale and exhale—the actual meaning of the garden's Japanese name. This temple also claims the smallest *kare sansui* garden in Japan. Called Totekiko, this little strip featuring gravel and several small rocks expresses the truism that the stronger the force of a stone thrown into water, the larger the ripple.

The dry landscape garden most familiar to people both inside and outside Japan is surely that of Ryoan-ji temple, created near the close of the fifteenth century. It comprises fifteen stones in five groupings, but no more than fourteen can be seen at once from any particular location on the viewing veranda (except perhaps at the moment of enlightenment, it has been suggested). This garden is exemplary of the principles of occult balance and of the concept of *ma:* negative space, or seemingly "empty" background, as an important part of an artistic composition. It is the *kare sansui* genre at its absolute purest. When Western visitors "discovered" this garden's existence in the early decades of the twentieth century they were stunned, for such a garden concept was elsewhere unheard of and beyond facile comprehension. When abstraction later became an important movement in Western art, it emerged as apparent that it was already a very old concept for the Japanese.

The imperial sites in the old capital offer impressive garden experiences on a much grander scale. The Kyoto Gosho imperial palace served as the emperor's official residence, with some interruptions, from 1331 to 1868, at which time the imperial seat was relocated to Tokyo. The forecourt of its Ceremonial Hall of State is a *yuniwa* sacred garden space paved simply in ancient style with crushed white rock, ornamented solely by a cherry tree and a *tachibana* mandarin orange tree flanking the entrance. In centuries past, Oike-no-Niwa, the palace's "Pond Garden," was a favored setting for elegant imperial parties.

At the inception of the Edo period (1603–1867), marked by the establishment of Tokugawa shogunal rule centered in Edo, former Tokyo, Nijo-jo castle was built as the Kyoto residence for the founder of that dynasty, Ieyasu. Ninomaru Palace was built on the grounds in the graceful *shoin-zukuri* study-room style favored by samurai of the time. It was given a pond garden with islands representing Horai, the "Islands of the Immortals" of Chinese legend, as well as the classic Crane and Tortoise islands typical of the historical Chinese inspiration from which Japanese gardens evolved. Its design is credited to the renowned garden master, architect, tea master, calligrapher, and poet of the day, Kobori Enshu. The abundance of stones, a predominant feature of this garden, was a predilection of Japan's warrior class to which Ieyasu belonged. A similar feature can also be seen in the garden at the Sambo-in subtemple of Daigo-ji, the renovation of which warlord and unifier of Japan Toyotomi Hideyoshi had sponsored not long before. The more than seven hundred stones displayed at Sambo-

in stood as an expression of the power of Hideyoshi, just as the palace garden stones did for Ieyasu.

Sento Gosho imperial retirement palace, with its surrounding gardens, was built in 1630 for retired emperor Go-Mizuno-o, who, in fact, had taken as consort Ieyasu's granddaughter. A man of refined taste and talents, he took a strong hand in the garden's design, alongside Kobori Enshu. On the grounds were two palaces, his own and Omiya Gosho for his empress. Both burned several times during the following two centuries and were rebuilt each time but the last, when only Omiya Gosho arose again for a later dowager empress. The magnificent twenty-two acres of gardens, however, still surround the North and South ponds, with strolling paths that employ appealing "hide and reveal" techniques. The shore of the South Pond is paved with river stones, said to number 111,000. Gathered at the behest of a provincial daimyo by his lieges, each stone found in suitable shape and size was paid for with a small measure of rice. The collection was formally presented at the palace as a gift, each one individually wrapped in silk.

A few years later Go-mizuno-o turned his attentions to the planning of his Shugaku-in Rikyu imperial villa in the northeastern hills. During the planning and construction phases he is said to have made visits to the site disguised in women's veiled travel attire to avoid the formality and protocol that would otherwise have been required. The vast naturalistic gardens of this country retreat are arranged around villas, pavilions, and teahouses on three elevations, providing a spectacular vista from the top that incorporates the distant mountains, in what is one of the most dramatic examples of the popular *shakkei* technique of bringing "borrowed scenery" from outside a garden's boundaries into its design. Of course, a legion of gardeners is required to tend such a vast and important property. Exemplary of the exacting and patient attention given to even the smallest of details is the sight of them perched in the pines, maintaining the impeccable appearance of the trees by plucking any unsightly brown needles from the branches.

Among Kyoto's imperial properties, it seems that one is more wonderful than the last. And so it is that Katsura Rikyu imperial villa, standing along the Katsura River in western Kyoto, is often called the epitome of Japanese architecture and garden arts. The property was a gift from the second Tokugawa shogun to an imperial prince, Hachijo-no-Miya Toshihito, and he and, later, his second son developed the villa and gardens between 1616 and 1660. Created around a large boating pond, this splendid stroll garden set on seventeen acres provides a multiplicity of views as one progresses along the deeply indented and twisting shoreline, crosses bridges, and passes tea arbors with poetic names like "Pine Zithern Pavilion" and "Moon Wave Pavilion." The villa itself is a staggered arrangement of linked structures, a Japanese architectural pattern known as "geese in flight," with the simplest materials used—wood, paper, straw—and the finest craftsmanship employed. German architect Bruno Taut, visiting this place in the 1930s, wrote in his diary that he was nearly moved to tears by its beauty. Initially through his efforts, after having already stood for roughly three centuries, Katsura Rikyu began to be known abroad.

When people consider the gardens of Japan, Tokyo rarely comes to mind, yet today's capital city possesses a number of resplendent examples—no longer situated at the city's edge as they originally were but now like oases squeezed into the middle of a huge metropolis. Edo was a rough-and-tumble city in comparison to Kyoto and was lacking in sophisticated cultural amenities. Early in the seventeenth century Tokugawa Yorifusa, Ieyasu's youngest son, was given a piece of land by the ruling Tokugawa shogun, Iemitsu, who was also Yorifusa's nephew. The plan was to create a suitable tea garden that could be used to entertain important guests of the shogunate outside the walls of the Edo Castle fortress. Acquiring still more land,

Yorifusa's idea expanded to a grand landscape garden, the likes of which had never been built in this young city. Its stroll circuit would eventually take in myriad sights styled in miniature after famous beauty spots of both Japan and of China. Further elaborated after his death by his son, with the aid of a Chinese Confucian scholar, it was named Koraku-en, "Garden of Later Pleasure," a name inspired by a Chinese saying that "the lord must bear sorrow before the people, and take pleasure after them." Today the still-large garden, called Koishikawa Koraku-en, is only a quarter of its original size, yet that it has survived the onslaught of urban expansion at all is to be greatly appreciated.

That sentiment also holds true for other historical gardens of Tokyo that have been revived and offered to posterity for continuing enjoyment in the heart of the city. Rikugi-en was designed around an island-dotted lake and comprised eighty-eight miniature landscape scenes from ancient Japanese and Chinese literature pleasingly arranged about the grounds. Although originally built at the beginning of the eighteenth century by a counselor of the shogun, it was bought and rehabilitated by Mitsubishi founder Baron Yataro Iwasaki in the early Meiji period (1868–1912). The wonderful Kiyosumi Gardens came into his ownership too, after the fortunes of its first owner dwindled. There he added a pond by diverting water from the Sumida River and collected countless noteworthy rocks for its enhancement from all across the country conveniently transporting them to Tokyo as ballast on his company's ships. Among them are impressive gatherings of huge stepping stones for Kiyosumi's beautiful water paths.

Provincial daimyo, who were required by the shogunate to spend part of each year in Edo, carried their garden memories and inspirations back home with them to create suitably beautiful and impressive gardens in their own fiefs. In Takamatsu on the island of Shikoku, the garden at Ritsurin-so was under construction for nearly one hundred years by successive daimyo of the Matsudaira family. Finally completed in the mid-eighteenth century, it remained in the family as an estate garden and duck-hunting grounds until the end of the feudal era, a little more than a century later, when it was opened to the public as Ritsurin Koen park.

Its spacious pine-studded grounds are faultlessly set against the forested backdrop of Mt. Shiun. A manmade waterfall on the mountainside recalls how, once upon a time, servants are said to have lugged barrels of water up the mountain so that, whenever the lord happened to pass that spot, they could cause water to cascade down for his pleasure. Lakes, ponds, and streams are lined with, and connected by, serpentine strolling paths. From the "Moon-Scooping Pavilion," a teahouse whose name was inspired by a Chinese poem, splendid views open onto the waters of South Lake with its picturesque bridge. On full-moon nights, trying to scoop that pearly reflection from the water was a delightful diversion for the family and guests. Lords of those days, when visiting each other, customarily exchanged particularly fine specimens of trees or rocks, and this unforgettable garden holds many such impressive gifts within its design.

Set on an islet nestled into a curve of Okayama's Asahi River is the superlative daimyo garden also known, like the Tokyo garden, as Koraku-en. At the time it was built, however, during the last years of the sixteenth century, its owner Lord Ikeda named it Chaya Yashiki, "Teahouse Estate." Replete with broad lawn-covered expanses and winding waterways, and an open layout of scenic promenades, the garden has several ponds, the largest of which features three islands and is said to mimic the scenery of Japan's largest lake, Lake Biwa. An interesting element of Korakuen is the paired "male" and "female" rocks here and there around the grounds, symbolizing the wish for fertility, reminding us that in those days male heirs were essential for the lord and his family to hold onto both power and property.

Okayama Castle is situated just across the river on a bluff, reachable by bridge. Castle inhabitants were able to gaze down onto the garden from above, while the castle has always offered impressive "borrowed scenery," adding content, depth, and atmosphere to the view from the garden. Although it suffered from bombing during the Second World War—not the only Japanese garden to do so—it was faithfully restored to its full beauty with the guidance of paintings and drawings from the Ikeda family archives.

In Kumamoto on the island of Kyushu stands an interesting garden begun by the third Hosokawa daimyo as a tea retreat in the seventeenth century. His son and grandson continued the work he started, finally completing it some eighty years after its inception. Called Suizen-ji Joju-en, for the Suizen-ji temple that the lord had built there a few years before starting the garden and for the secular pleasure garden Joju-en it later became when the temple was replaced with a teahouse brought from Katsura Rikyu, the garden centers on a pond fed by a subterranean stream flowing from the nearby volcanic Mt. Aso. A half-hour stroll along garden paths leads the viewer past visual references to the fifty-three post stations of the old Tokaido, the scenic "Eastern Sea Road" that connected Edo with Kyoto in those times. Some of the scenes are recognizable to knowledgeable Japanese visitors, while others are more obscure, but the one scene recognizable to all is the graceful, grass-covered miniature re-creation of Mt. Fuji.

These gardens are inspired by nature but seem to be beyond nature, are inspired by religious faith but stand beyond religion. Transcending time, the gardens of the past are equally gardens of today, for as the author of the *Sakuteiki* concluded already in the eleventh century, "the spirit of the garden is inexhaustible." To the connoisseur and uninitiated alike, Japanese gardens offer magical revelations and inspirations. Visitors can lose themselves not only in their incomparable beauty but in engaging garden tales that delineate a splendid culture stretching far back through time.

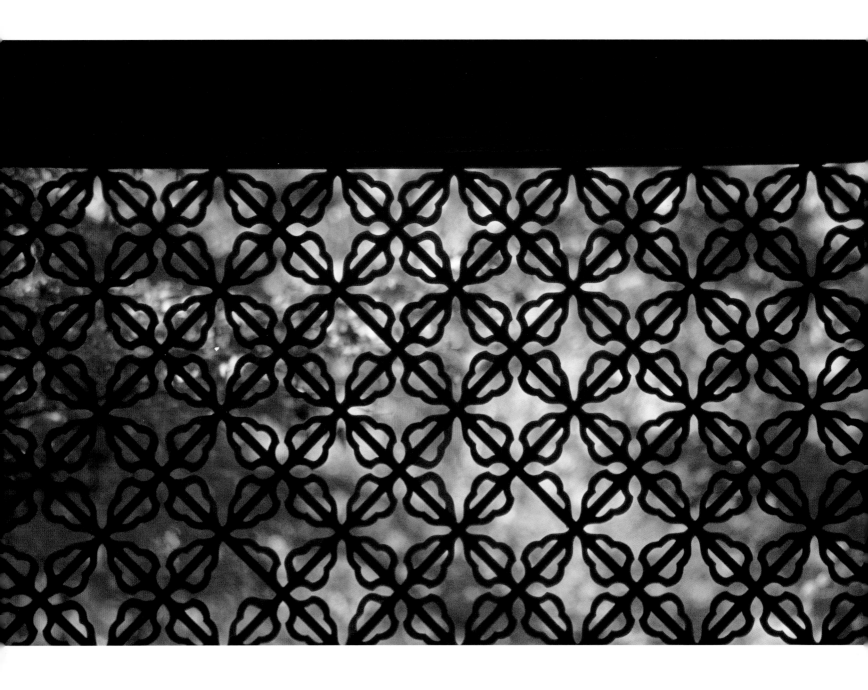

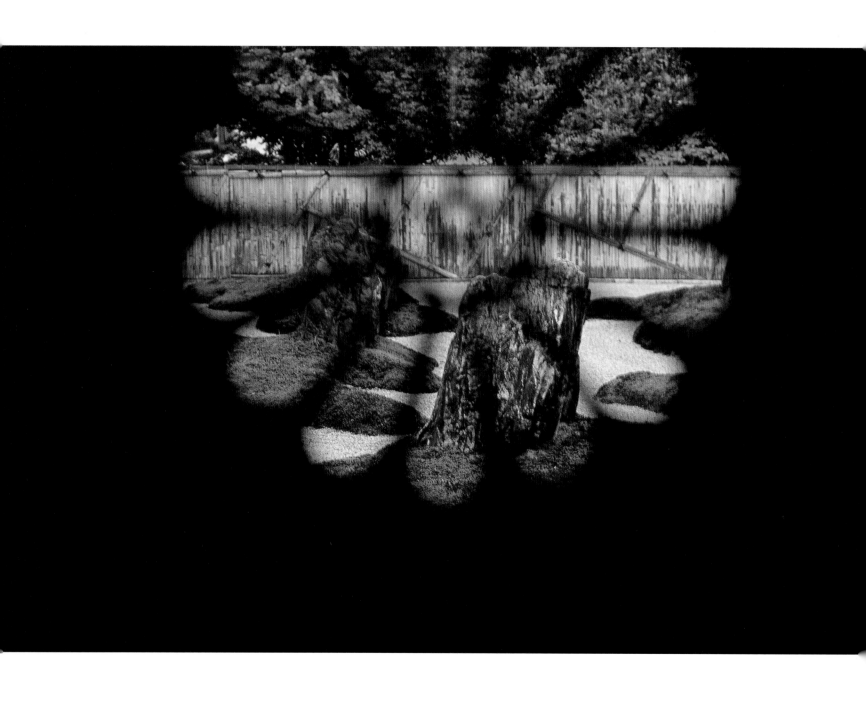

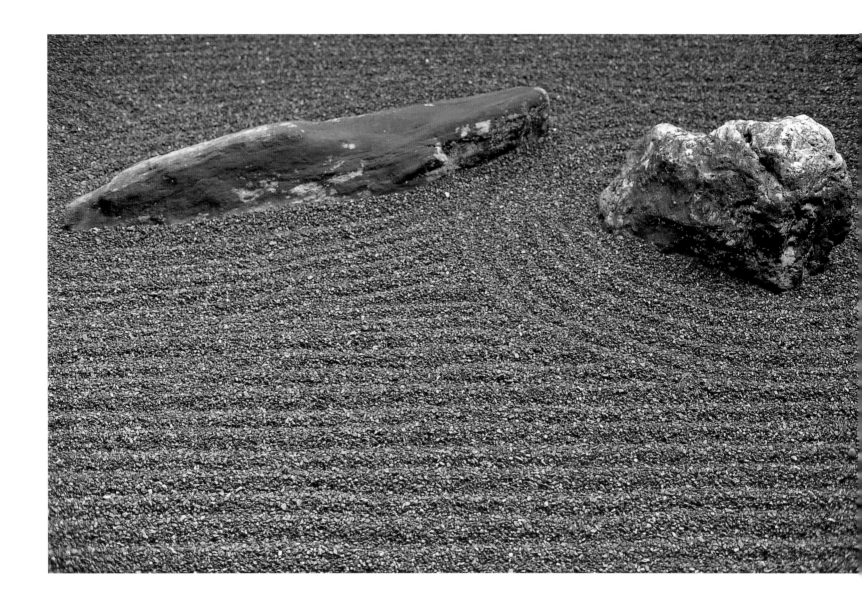

TOKYO

BE

Captions

Numbers indicate pages.

Front Cover

Mirei Shigemori Garden Museum, Kyoto

Back Cover

Abbot's Hall south garden, Tofuku-ji temple, Kyoto

KYOTO

14-15

Mirei Shigemori Garden Museum
The Mirei Shigemori Garden Museum, former home of the twentieth-century master, features his Muji-an garden of moss and stone.

16

Matsuno-o Taisha
The "Winding Stream Garden" at Matsuno-o Taisha shrine is a bold composition of stone, water, and bushes, designed by Mirei Shigemori.

17

Matsuno-o Taisha
Garden master Mirei Shigemori set a handsome stone slab to bridge the shores in the "Winding Stream Garden" at Matsuno-o Taisha shrine.

18

Matsuno-o Taisha
A grouping of rocks, suggesting a sacred *iwakura*, abode of the gods, makes up Mirei Shigemori's "Garden of Ancient Times" at Matsuno-o Taisha shrine.

19

Matsuno-o Taisha
Mirei Shigemori's "Horai Garden" at Matsuno-o-Taisha shrine represents the legendary "Islands of the Immortals" of Chinese Taoist tradition.

20

Sanzen-in
Water trickles through a bamboo pipe into an old stone water basin nestled among fallen leaves at Sanzen-in temple in Ohara.

21

Kozan-ji
The ornamental woodwork of the Sekisui-in study hall of Kozan-ji temple is outlined against fiery maple trees in the garden.

22

Tofuku-ji
At Tofuku-ji temple, a checkerboard-patterned garden is styled from moss and recycled paving stones in accord with the Zen precept against waste.

23

Shinnyo-in
At Shinnyo-in temple, flat river stones laid in an overlapping pattern create the remarkable impression of a flowing stream.

24

Kinkaku-ji
The "Golden Pavilion" is the focal point of a splendid five-century-old pond garden at Kinkaku-ji temple, formerly a shogunal retirement estate.

25

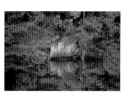

Kinkaku-ji
Mirror Pond at the Kinkaku-ji temple reflects the profuse greenery and rockwork along the shore and on its many islets.

26

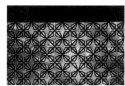

Eikan-do Zenrin-ji
A blaze of autumn color sets off the decorative openwork of the *karamon* Chinese-style gate at Eikan-do Zenrin-ji temple.

27

Eikan-do Zenrin-ji
A resplendent red maple tree in the garden of Eikan-do Zenrin-ji temple stands framed within a *katomado,* a "flame," or "bud," window.

28

Ryogen-in (Daitoku-ji)
The Isshidan dry landscape garden at Ryogen-in temple features symbolic mountains and islands in a sea of white gravel.

29

Myoman-ji
A Buddhist monk rakes representative patterns in the sand at Myoman-ji temple's *kare sansui* dry landscape garden.

30

Renge-ji
A stone lantern is framed by a profusion of autumn color around Renge-ji temple's pond garden, dating from the seventeenth century.

31

Tenryu-ji
The pond garden at the Zen temple Tenryu-ji was designed by the temple's talented first abbot, Muso Soseki, in the fourteenth century.

32
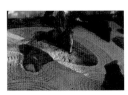

Mirei Shigemori Garden Museum
Moss and rock islands are set amid the raked gravel "waters" of the Muji-an garden at the Mirei Shigemori Garden Museum.

33

Mirei Shigemori Garden Museum
A stream of raked gravel is bordered by a free-form pavement of red granite below the veranda at the Mirei Shigemori Garden Museum.

34

Ginkaku-ji
The Ginshadan, an abstract dry landscape garden at Ginkaku-ji temple, represents a broad sea of silver sand.

35

Ginkaku-ji
The focus of the sand garden at Ginkaku-ji temple, the Kogetsudai mound, has been likened to Mt. Fuji, and the circle of its truncation to the full moon.

36
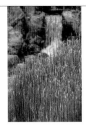

Seiryu-en (Nijo-jo)
Beyond a bed of rushes, water cascades into the pond at Seiryu-en, the "Clear Stream Garden" on the grounds of the Nijo-jo castle complex.

37

Zenno-ji (Sennyu-ji)
A multitude of striking rocks are arranged beneath shade trees in the "Garden of Peace for the Departed" at Zenno-ji temple.

38

Seiryu-en (Nijo-jo)
Seiryu-en garden was created within the Nijo-jo castle compound in 1965 as a venue for large tea parties and official Kyoto receptions.

39

Seiryu-en (Nijo-jo)
At Seiryu-en garden, the pond shores are paved with river stones and studded with rocks acquired from a historic Kyoto villa and elsewhere in Japan.

40

Tofuku-ji

An eighteenth-century *kare sansui* garden, raked in an *ichimatsu* checkerboard pattern, stands alongside Tofuku-ji's "Founder's Hall."

41

Ryosoku-in (Kennin-ji)

A sand cone in the garden at Ryosoku-in temple represents Shumisen, or Mt. Sumeru, the center of the world according to Buddhist cosmology.

42

Ryogen-in (Daitoku-ji)

Totekiko, said to be the smallest rock garden in Japan, is framed by dramatic shadows between walls at Ryogen-in temple.

43

Honen-in

Fresh camellia blossoms grace a *tsukubai* water basin at Honen-in temple, known for its camellia garden.

44

Shisen-do

A clump of *tokusa* rushes thrives along a rivulet flowing through the garden to a small pond at the former villa, Shisen-do.

45

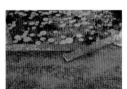

Hompo-ji

A water lily pond, framed by cut stones arranged to form a decagon, stands in the Mitsudomoe-no-Niwa garden at Hompo-ji temple.

46

Daisen-in (Daitoku-ji)

Water flowing beneath a bridge is represented with raked gravel and stone in the *kare sansui* garden, built in 1509, at Daisen-in temple.

47

Daisen-in (Daitoku-ji)

The Tiger's Head stone, symbolizing tragedy and confusion encountered in the river of life, is part of the *kare sansui* garden at Daisen-in temple.

48

Kingyu-in (Myoshin-ji)

A branch of a pine tree is weighted with an *omoshi* stone to train it to the desired aesthetic position at Kingyu-in temple.

49

Ryogin-an (Tofuku-ji)

Autumn leaves accent the modernist *kare sansui* garden featuring stones set into contrasting shades of gravel at Ryogin-an temple.

50

Saiho-ji
Saiho-ji temple is popularly known as Koke-dera, the "Moss Temple," for its exceptional garden carpeted in more than a hundred kinds of moss.

51

Saiho-ji
The garden at Saiho-ji temple dates from the fourteenth century, but the profusion of mosses has only slowly taken possession over the ages.

52

Kosei-ji
The "Peaceful Heart Garden" of Kosei-ji temple can be seen through the chrysanthemum-shaped openwork in a garden gate.

53

Mirei Shigemori Garden Museum
A rope-tied barrier stone in the Muji-an garden at the Mirei Shigemori Garden Museum reminds visitors they may not step beyond that point.

54

Ryogin-an (Tofuku-ji)
"The Garden of the Inseparable" at Ryogin-an temple is an arrangement of stones on a bed of red sand, depicting a legend about the thirteenth-century temple founder.

55

Ryogin-an (Tofuku-ji)
The founder of Ryogin-an temple is said to have been abandoned in the mountains as a child, and two of the stones in the garden's design symbolize a dog protecting him.

56

Shosei-en (Higashi Hongan-ji)
A Chinese-style corridor bridge spans a pond inlet at the seventeenth-century Shosei-en garden, where once an early Heian-era garden stood.

57

Honen-in
Water trickles from a stone basin over a leaf, plucked daily by the gardener from a camellia tree in the garden of Honen-in temple.

58

Yoshimine-dera
The "Gliding Dragon Pine" at Yoshimine-dera temple is a natural monument six hundred years old, trained horizontally to a length of forty-two meters.

59

Sento Gosho
A caretaker rakes the shore of the North Pond in the seventeenth-century gardens of the onetime Sento Gosho imperial palace.

60

Heian Jingu
Pillars salvaged from two earthquake-damaged city bridges were reused to create stepping stones across the garden pond at Heian Jingu shrine.

61

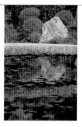

Kaizan-do (Tofuku-ji)
A stone bridge crosses the pond in front of the Kaizan-do, or "Founder's Hall," at Tofuku-ji, a Zen temple possessing a wealth of gardens.

62

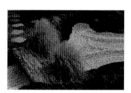

Zuiho-in (Daitoku-ji)
A stone slab bridge spans the symbolic waters of the "Garden of Solitary Meditation," one of three gardens at Zuiho-in temple.

63

Zuiho-in (Daitoku-ji)
A single stone marks the distant sea of deeply raked gravel on the east side of the "Garden of Solitary Meditation" at Zuiho-in temple.

64

Zuiho-in (Daitoku-ji)
Stepping stones cross Zuiho-in temple's "Quietly Sleeping Garden," leading to a bamboo gate and a teahouse behind the hedge.

65

Reiun-in (Tofuku-ji)
In the garden of Reiun-in temple, a unique stone representing Mount Shumisen, the center of the Buddhist cosmos, is set on a pedestal.

66

Sanzen-in
Sekisho, so-called sweet rushes, flourish around a stone water basin in the garden of Sanzen-in temple in Ohara.

67

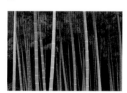

Saiho-ji
A grove of towering bamboo is part of the garden of Saiho-ji, a Zen temple built on the site of a seventh-century princely estate.

68

Shosei-en (Higashi Hongan-ji)
An artful wall at Shosei-en garden was constructed of stones salvaged from Higashi Hongan-ji temple following a nineteenth-century fire.

69

Sento Gosho
Myriad beach stones paving the South Pond shore in the Sento Gosho imperial palace gardens were a onetime gift from a provincial daimyo to the emperor.

70

Sento Gosho
A stone lantern is nestled beneath the trees near the shore of the South Pond at the seventeenth-century Sento Gosho imperial palace gardens.

71

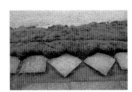

Tenju-an (Nanzen-ji)
A stone footpath of geometric design borders the moss edging the *kare sansui* garden at Tenju-an temple.

72

Musha-no-Koji Senke
Moss encroaches on a path composed of Oribe-gawara tiles glistening in the rain in the tea garden at Musha-no-Koji Senke tea school.

73

Hosen-in
Exemplary of Buddhist-Shinto syncretism, sacred sand cones provide places for the native Shinto gods to alight at Hosen-in temple in Ohara.

74

Shugaku-in Rikyu
A heron perches on a stone-slab bridge in the naturalistic grounds of the seventeenth-century Shugaku-in Rikyu imperial villa.

75

Shugaku-in Rikyu
A wooden boat is moored in its boathouse at the edge of the "Bathing Dragon Pond" at Shugaku-in Rikyu imperial villa.

76

Shugaku-in Rikyu
The distant mountains seen from Shugaku-in Rikyu imperial villa exemplify the classic "borrowed scenery" design technique.

77

Daikaku-ji
At Daikaku-ji temple, pine trees stand on Chrysanthemum Island in the lotus-filled Osawa-no-Ike pond dating from the ninth century.

78

Tofuku-ji
Sunlight catches a spiral pattern representing one of the eight rough seas of life expressed in the raked sand garden of Tofuku-ji temple.

79

Tofuku-ji
Patterns and textures of stone and sand create a pleasing abstraction at the corner of a garden at Tofuku-ji temple.

80

Ninomaru Palace Garden (Nijo-jo)
The roseate Beni-Gamo Ishi is one of seven impressive Kamo River stones in the Ninomaru Palace Garden within the Nijo-jo castle complex.

81

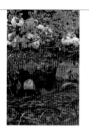

Ninomaru Palace Garden (Nijo-jo)
A *sato-zakura* cherry tree blossoms among the rockery of the Ninomaru Palace Garden in the Nijo-jo castle complex.

82

Reiun-in (Tofuku-ji)
Patterns of concentric circles are sculpted in two colors of sand in the modern "Quiet Clouds Garden" at Reiun-in temple.

83

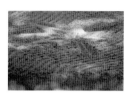

Honen-in
At Honen-in temple, dais-like sand beds just inside the temple gate are patterned with seasonal designs, such as this autumn maple leaf.

84

Ikkyu-ji
Rocks in the garden of Ikkyu-ji temple are said to symbolize the sixteen disciples of Buddha amid a landscape of mountains, valleys, and a waterfall.

85

Musha-no-Koji Senke
At Musha-no-Koji Senke tea school, charcoal is embedded along the edge of the garden's moss to absorb damaging excess moisture.

86

Sanzen-in
A stone statue of the bodhisattva Jizo stands in the naturalistic Yusei-en, "Garden of Pure Presence," at Sanzen-in temple.

87

Sanzen-in
Shuheki-en, the "Garden of Gathering of Deep Green" at Sanzen-in temple, features a stone pagoda surrounded by rocks, moss, and trimmed bushes.

88

Hogon-in (Tenryu-ji)
A magnificent "nightingale" fence, intricately woven of untrimmed bamboo branches, stands against the autumn maples at Hogon-in temple.

89

Sanzen-in
Fallen maple leaves cling to the handcrafted bamboo cover of a spring-fed well in the garden of Sanzen-in temple in Ohara.

90

Kanchi-in (To-ji)
The *kare sansui* garden at Kanchi-in temple honors Kukai, also known as Kobo Daishi, the ninth-century monk, scholar, poet, calligrapher, and the founder of Shingon Buddhism.

91

Kanchi-in (To-ji)
The raked patterns in the garden at Kanchi-in temple represent the perilous sea across which Kukai returned after his studies in China, while the stones tell the legend of that voyage.

92

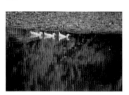

Ryoan-ji
At Ryoan-ji temple, ducks paddle across the Mirror Pond, which was once a part of a Heian-period aristocratic estate garden.

93

Sanzen-in
A wood-and-stone lantern pierced with a crescent moon design stands beneath the trees in the Yusei-en garden at Sanzen-in temple.

94

Katsura Rikyu
Ama-no-Hashidate, a place of scenic beauty on the Sea of Japan, is symbolically recreated within the gardens of Katsura Rikyu imperial villa.

95

Ninomaru Palace Garden (Nijo-jo)
Fallen autumn leaves mass along the stone-lined pond embankment in the Ninomaru Palace Garden in the Nijo-jo castle complex.

96

Ninomaru Palace Garden (Nijo-jo)
Water fed from the adjacent inner moat of Nijo-jo castle cascades into the pond in the Ninomaru Palace garden.

97

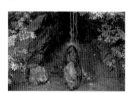

Kinkaku-ji
The "Carp Stone" in the garden of Kinkaku-ji temple represents the Chinese legend of a carp swimming up a waterfall to gain dragonhood.

98

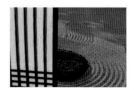

Kennin-ji
Beyond the paper *shoji* of Kennin-ji temple's abbot's quarters lies the bold dry landscape design of the "Garden of Grandeur."

99

Kennin-ji
While Kennin-ji, founded in 1202, is the oldest Zen temple in Kyoto, its modernist "Garden of Grandeur" was created in the twentieth century.

100

Ginkaku-ji
A sinuous path of broom-raked sand leads to a stone-slab bridge in the stroll garden of Ginkaku-ji, the "Silver Pavilion."

101

Ryoan-ji
A rock grouping in the austere fifteenth-century raked sand garden of Ryoan-ji temple stands against the weathered oil-clay garden wall.

102

Kaju-ji
The decorative base of an old toppled lantern remains on the boat landing of the ancient pond garden at Kaju-ji temple.

103

Shobo-ji
Around the lush pond and adjoining dry landscape garden at Shobo-ji temple, many rocks are thought to resemble various birds and animals.

TOKYO

104-105

Koishikawa Koraku-en
The arcs of a bamboo fence at the edge of a pond at Koishikawa Koraku-en seem to reflect the scalloped appearance of a nearby pine tree.

106

Shinjuku Gyoen
A sculpted pine grows at the edge of a pond in the Japanese garden within the vast grounds of Shinjuku Gyoen park.

107

Koishikawa Koraku-en
At Koishikawa Koraku-en, an Edo-era stroll garden, a stone-slab bridge spans the Inner Garden water lily pond from the shore to its island.

108

Shinjuku Gyoen
A stone lantern stands against the backdrop of Kami-no-Ike Pond and its "Drum Bridge" in the Japanese garden at Shinjuku Gyoen park.

109

Shinjuku Gyoen
An ornamental cluster of clouds is carved on a towering stone lantern in the Japanese garden at Shinjuku Gyoen park.

110

Rikugi-en
A stone lantern, set among trees in the seventeenth-century stroll garden Rikugi-en, is cast into high contrast in the late afternoon light.

111

Koishikawa Koraku-en
The centuries-old *hitotsu matsu,* "single pine," with its snaking trunk and branches, stands at the edge of Daisensui pond at Koishikawa Koraku-en.

112

Rikugi-en
Two elliptical stone slabs are counterpoised to form the distinctive "Moon-Crossing Bridge" leading to an island in the pond at Rikugi-en.

113

Shinjuku Gyoen
A stone lantern top is styled to suggest a sacred Buddhist treasure gem called *hoju* in the Japanese garden at Shinjuku Gyoen park.

114

Dembo-in (Senso-ji)
The celebrated pagoda at Senso-ji temple in Asakusa is reflected in the garden pond of the nearby abbot's quarters, Dembo-in.

115

Kiyosumi Teien
Stepping stones called *iso watari,* accented by a clump of blooming *susuki* grass, lead across the pond shallows at Kiyosumi Teien.

116

Kiyosumi Teien
In a corner of Kiyosumi Teien stands a stone inscribed with a *haiku* by seventeenth-century poet Basho: "Old pond/frog jumps in/sound of water."

117

Kyu Shiba Rikyu Onshi Teien
A fine old "snow-viewing" stone lantern stands at the edge of the spring-fed pond at Kyu Shiba Rikyu Onshi Teien, the Shiba Detached Palace garden.

118

Kiyosumi Teien
Stepping stones form a pond crossing at Kiyosumi Teien, an Edo-era stroll garden renowned for its superb collection of stones from all over Japan.

119

Kiyosumi Teien
A splendid veined stone from the island of Shikoku is set prominently at the head of a stepping-stone path hugging the shore of the pond at Kiyosumi Teien.

120

Kyu Yasuda Teien
The pond at Kyu Yasuda Teien is fed from the Sumida River near Tokyo Bay, so its level ebbs and flows with the tides.

121

Happo-en
A small rustic pavilion stands in a quiet arbor at the edge of the pond at the Edo-period garden Happo-en in Shirokanedai.

122

Kiyosumi Teien
A sculptural black stone, one of countless splendid specimens collected from all over Japan by the onetime owner of the garden, is set in the pond at Kiyosumi Teien.

123

Kyu Furukawa Teien
A striking bridge crafted from a pair of massive stone slabs spans Shinji Ike pond in the Japanese woodland garden of Kyu Furukawa Teien.

124

Kyu Furukawa Teien
A handsome lantern stands on the pebble-paved shore of Shinji Ike pond in the twentieth-century Taisho-period garden, Kyu Furukawa Teien.

125

Joren-ji
The small garden pond at Joren-ji temple, home to the Tokyo Great Buddha, teems with *koi*, highly collectible ornamental carp.

126

Chidorigafuchi
The view from the Chidorigafuchi promenade across the moat to the imperial palace grounds is glorious during the spring cherry blossom season.

127

Shinjuku Gyoen
Friends enjoy *o-hanami,* a spring blossom-viewing party, beneath the blooming cherry trees of Shinjuku Gyoen park.

128

Koishikawa Koraku-en
Byobu iwa, tall rocks suggesting a traditional Japanese folding screen, stand beyond an artfully paved pond bank at Koishikawa Koraku-en.

129

Koishikawa Koraku-en
The shade-dappled waters of Koishikawa Koraku-en's west pond are crossed by a staggered path of mushroom-shaped stepping stones.

130

Meiji Jingu
On a rainy day, a couple strolls through Meiji Jingu shrine's iris garden, designed by Emperor Meiji himself for his wife, Empress Shoken.

131

Meiji Jingu
A painter in traditional sunbonnet, one of many artists who come to Meiji Jingu shrine's iris garden, captures the beauty of the blossoms on canvas.

132

Rikugi-en
Tsuru-no-Bashi, the earth-covered Crane Bridge edged with grass, links the shore of Rikugi-en's pond to Naka-no-Shima island.

133

Rikugi-en
A collection of irregularly shaped stepping stones creates a modernistic path across the moss at three-hundred-year-old Rikugi-en.

134

Shinobazu Pond (Ueno Onshi Koen)
Lotus plants flourish in the immense Shinobazu Pond in Ueno Onshi Koen park during the heat of summer, creating a spot of urban coolness.

135

Koishikawa Koraku-en
Hills planted with bamboo grass, representing the scenic Chinese mountain Ro-zan, rise behind a lotus pond at Koishikawa Koraku-en garden.

136

Shinjuku Gyoen
Taiko Bashi, the "Drum Bridge," spans the waters of the Upper Pond in Shinjuku Gyoen park's traditional Japanese stroll garden.

137

Shinjuku Gyoen
An assemblage of natural stones creates a rustic lantern set beneath the trees in the Japanese garden at Shinjuku Gyoen park.

138

Kiyosumi Teien
Black river stones brought from Izu Peninsula form delineating patterns between large stepping stones at Kiyosumi Teien.

139

Koishikawa Koraku-en
A path of rounded stepping stones crosses a walkway paved with river stones in the seventeenth-century Koishikawa Koraku-en stroll garden.

BEYOND

140-141

Raikyu-ji
An undulating pattern symbolizes the rolling sea in the four-century-old Raikyu-ji temple garden at Bitchu-Takahashi, Okayama.

142

Adachi Museum of Art
Like the framed art within the Adachi Museum in Yasugi, Shimane, the museum's gardens can also be viewed within the frames of the building's apertures.

143

Adachi Museum of Art
The founder of the Adachi Museum collected countless pine trees and rocks from all over Japan to complete the vast surrounding gardens.

144

Kinchakuda
Beneath the trees at Kinchakuda in Hidaka, Saitama, autumn-blooming spider lilies called *higan-bana*, or "equinox flowers," carpet the field.

145

Daichi-ji
Sculpted azalea hedges represent the treasure ship of the "Seven Lucky Gods" sailing a sea of raked sand at Daichi-ji temple in Minakuchi, Shiga.

146

Tsuki-no-Katsura-no-Niwa
The splendid Tsuki-no-Katsura-no-Niwa, a private family garden in Yamaguchi, was created in 1712 as an homage to the moon and fertility.

147

Tsuki-no-Katsura-no-Niwa
The centerpiece of Tsuki-no-Katsura-no-Niwa is an unusual stone symbolizing a hare impregnated by moonlight, after a Chinese Buddhist tale.

148

Meigetsu-in
Every June, some three thousand hydrangea bushes come into bloom at Kamakura's Meigetsu-in, popularly known as the "Hydrangea Temple."

149

Meigetsu-in
Hydrangea blossoms are heaped into the lap of a stone Jizo bodhisattva figure as an offering at Meigetsu-in temple.

150

Koraku-en
Okayama Castle comprises an element of "borrowed scenery" for its daimyo stroll garden, Koraku-en, set on a river island below its ramparts.

151

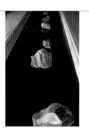

Koraku-en
Koraku-en's Ryuten Pavilion, with a stream channeled through and set with stones, provided a resting place for the onetime daimyo on his garden strolls.

152

Koraku-en
A solitary lantern stands at the curve of a watercourse flowing through the expansive grounds of Koraku-en garden in Okayama.

153

Koraku-en
Kilometers of paths, crossing streams and encircling ponds, weave through Okayama's four-century-old Koraku-en garden.

154

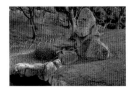

Koraku-en
Fertility stones, standing in pairs and representing the elements of *yin* and *yang*, are a particular feature of Koraku-en garden in Okayama.

155

Koraku-en
Koraku-en garden's own crane aviary assures that, once again, red-crowned *tancho* are a common sight here as they were from the garden's inception.

156

Koraku-en
A pine bough grown to extravagant length extends over a pond in the four-century-old daimyo stroll garden, Koraku-en, in Okayama.

157

Koraku-en
A placid waterway reflects garden strollers and the twilight sky at Koraku-en in Okayama, one of Japan's most famous gardens.

158

Suizen-ji
A representation of Mount Fuji is one of fifty-three scenic views recreated at the Suizen-ji Joju-en stroll garden in Kumamoto, Kyushu.

159

Ryuge-ji
Densely planted shrubs and trees cover the slope of the "Fuji View Garden," Kanfu-en, at Ryuge-ji temple in Shimizu-ku, Shizuoka.

Isui-en
A footpath crossing the pond at Isui-en garden in Nara is styled from old millstones once used to grind *soba*, or buckwheat.

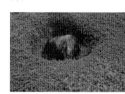

Mori-shi Teien
A stone is framed by a round of sculpted shrubbery in Mori-shi Teien, the "Lord Mori Garden," built in Hofu, Yamaguchi, in the early twentieth century.

Rinno-ji
A stone lantern overgrown with moss and greenery stands in the Edo-era stroll garden Shoyo-en at Rinno-ji temple in Nikko.

Rinno-ji
Moss covers a bridge fashioned from a pair of staggered stone bars in the stroll garden Shoyo-en at Rinno-ji temple in Nikko.

Ohori Koen
Stepping stones cross the rocky shore of the Japanese garden pond at Ohori Koen park in Fukuoka, on the island of Kyushu.

Ohori Koen
The pond waters of the pine-studded Japanese garden of Ohori Koen park are drawn from what was once the "great moat," or *ohori*, defending Fukuoka Castle.

Ryotan-ji
Hills, stones, and clipped azalea bushes evoke the Taoist "Islands of the Immortals" in a pond garden at Ryotan-ji temple in Inasa-cho, Shizuoka.

Ritsurin Koen
A cherry tree in full bloom adds to the grace of Engetsu-kyo, the "Full Moon Bridge," at Ritsurin Koen park in Takamatsu, Shikoku.

Ritsurin Koen
Pine trees are the centerpieces in the raked sand garden alongside the Kikugetsu-tei teahouse at Ritsurin Koen park in Takamatsu, Shikoku.

Ritsurin Koen
The open *shoji* paper doors of the "Moon-Scooping Pavilion" in Ritsurin Koen park reveal a serene view of South Lake.

170

Ritsurin Koen
A grey heron stands on the shore of South Lake in Ritsurin Koen park, the largest garden in Japan, on the island of Shikoku.

171

Ritsurin Koen
One of the finest stones at Ritsurin Koen park is the *botan-ishi,* "Peony Stone," set on Yoto Island in Kansui Pond.

172

Ritsurin Koen
Black pine trees stand like elaborate sculptures in many parts of the old daimyo garden that is now Ritsurin Koen park.

173

Ritsurin Koen
Garden greenery is framed within a round, latticed window called *yoshinomado* in the "Moon-Scooping Pavilion" at Ritsurin Koen park.

Locations

KYOTO

Daikaku-ji 大覚寺
4 Saga-osawa-cho, Ukyo-ku, Kyoto 616-8411
〒616-8411 京都市右京区嵯峨大沢町 4

Daisen-in 大徳寺大仙院
Murasakino-daitokuji-cho, Kita-ku, Kyoto 603-8231
〒603-8231 京都市北区紫野大徳寺町 54-1

Eikan-do Zenrin-ji 永観堂禅林寺
48 Eikando-cho, Sakyo-ku, Kyoto 606-8445
〒606-8445 京都市左京区永観堂町 48

Ginkaku-ji 銀閣寺 （慈照寺）
2 Ginkakuji-cho, Sakyo-ku, Kyoto 606-8402
〒606-8402 京都市左京区銀閣寺町 2

Heian Jingu 平安神宮
97 Okazaki-nishitenno-cho, Sakyo-ku, Kyoto 606-8341
〒606-8341 京都市左京区岡崎西天王町 97

Hogon-in 天龍寺 宝厳院
36 Saga-tenryuji-susukinobaba-cho, Ukyo-ku, Kyoto 616-8385
〒616-8385 京都市右京区嵯峨天龍寺芒ノ馬場町 36

Hompo-ji 本法寺
617 Hompojimae-cho, Ogawa-dori, Teranouchi-agaru, Kamigyo-ku, Kyoto 602-0061
〒602-0061 京都市上京区小川通寺之内上ル本法寺前町 617

Honen-in 法然院
30 Shishigatani-goshonodan-cho, Sakyo-ku, Kyoto 606-8422
〒606-8422 京都市左京区鹿ヶ谷御所ノ段町 30

Ikkyu-ji 一休寺 （酬恩庵）
102 Takigisatonouchi, Kyotanabe-shi, Kyoto 610-0341
〒610-0341 京田辺市薪里ノ内 102

Kaizan-do 東福寺 開山堂
15-778 Honmachi, Higashiyama-ku, Kyoto 607-605-0981
〒605-0981 京都市東山区本町 15-778

Kaju-ji 勧修寺
27-6 Kanshuji-niodo-cho, Yamashina-ku, Kyoto 607-8226
〒607-8226 京都市山科区勧修寺仁王堂町 27-6

Kanchi-in 東寺 観智院
403 Kujo-cho, Hachijo-omiya-nishi-iru, Minami-ku, Kyoto 601-8473
〒601-8473 京都市南区八条大宮西入ル九条町 403

Katsura Rikyu 桂離宮
Katsuramisono, Nishikyo-ku, Kyoto 615-8014
〒615-8014 京都市西京区桂御園

Kennin-ji 建仁寺
584 Komatsu-cho, Higashiyama-ku, Kyoto 605-0811
〒605-0811 京都市東山区小松町 584

Kingyu-in 妙心寺 金牛院
45 Hanazono-myoshinji-cho, Ukyo-ku, Kyoto 616-8035
〒616-8035 京都市右京区花園妙心寺町 45

Kinkaku-ji 金閣寺 （鹿苑寺）
1 Kinkakuji-cho, Kita-ku, Kyoto 603-8361
〒603-8361 京都市北区金閣寺町 1

Kosei-ji 光清寺
Shichiban-cho, Izumi-dori, Rokken-cho-nishi-iru, Kamigyo-ku, Kyoto 602-8359
〒602-8359 京都市上京区出水通六軒町西入ル七番町

Kozan-ji 高山寺 石水院
8 Umegahata-togano-o-cho, Ukyo-ku, Kyoto 616-8295
〒616-8295 京都市右京区梅ヶ畑栂尾町 8

Matsuno-o Taisha 松尾大社
3 Arashiyama-miyamachi, Nishikyo-ku, Kyoto 616-0024
〒616-0024 京都市西京区嵐山宮町 3

Mirei Shigemori Garden Museum 重森三玲庭園美術館
34 Yoshida-kamioji-cho, Sakyo-ku, Kyoto 606-8312
〒606-8312 京都市左京区吉田上大路町 34

Musha-no-Koji Senke 武者小路千家
613 Ogawa Higashi-hairu, Mushanokoji-dori, Kamigyo-ku, Kyoto 602-0936
〒602-0936 京都市上京区武者小路通り小川東入ル 613

Myoman-ji 妙満寺
91 Iwakura-hataeda-cho, Sakyo-ku, Kyoto 606-0015
〒606-0015 京都市左京区岩倉幡枝町 91

Ninomaru Palace Garden 二条城 二ノ丸庭園
541 Nijojo-cho, Nijo-dori, Horikawa-nishi-iru Nakagyo-ku, Kyoto 604-8301
〒604-8301 京都市中京区二条通堀川西入ル二条城町 541

Reiun-in 東福寺 霊雲院
15-801 Honmachi, Higashiyama-ku, Kyoto 605-0981
〒605-0981 京都市東山区本町 15-801

Renge-ji 蓮華寺
1 Kamitakano-hachiman-cho, Sakyo-ku, Kyoto 606-0065
〒606-0065 京都市左京区上高野八幡町 1

Ryoan-ji 龍安寺
13 Ryoanji-goryonoshita-machi, Ukyo-ku, Kyoto 616-8001
〒616-8001 京都市右京区龍安寺御陵ノ下町 13

Ryogen-in 大徳寺 龍源院
82-1 Murasakino-daitokuji-cho, Kita-ku, Kyoto 603-8231
〒603-8231 京都市北区紫野大徳寺町 82-1

Ryogin-an 東福寺 龍吟庵
15-812 Honmachi, Higashiyama-ku, Kyoto 605-0981
〒605-0981 京都市東山区本町 15-812

Ryosoku-in 建仁寺 両足院
591 Komatsu-cho, Higashiyama-ku, Kyoto 605-0811
〒605-0811 京都市東山区小松町 591

Saiho-ji 西芳寺 （苔寺）
56 Matsuo-jingatani-cho, Nishikyo-ku, Kyoto 615-8286
〒615-8286 京都市西京区松尾神ヶ谷町 56

Saio-in 金戒光明寺 西翁院
33 Kurodani-cho, Sakyo-ku, Kyoto 606-8331
〒606-8331 京都市左京区黒谷町 33

Sanzen-in 三千院
540 Ohara-raikoin-cho, Sakyo-ku, Kyoto 601-1242
〒601-1242 京都市左京区大原来迎院町 540

Seiryu-en 二条城 清流園
541 Nijojo-cho, Nijo-dori, Horikawa-nishi-iru Nakagyo-ku, Kyoto 604-8301
〒604-8301 京都市中京区二条通堀川西入ル二条城町 541

Sento Gosho 仙洞御所
3 Kyoto-gyoen, Kamigyo-ku, Kyoto 602-0881
〒602-0881 京都市上京区京都御苑 3 番

Shinnyo-in 真如院
677 Kakimoto-cho, Gojo-agaru, Inokuma-dori, Shimogyo-ku, Kyoto 600-8357
〒600-8357 京都市下京区猪熊通五条上ル柿本町 677

Shisen-do 詩仙堂
27 Ichijoji-monguchi-cho, Sakyo-ku, Kyoto 606-8154
〒606-8154 京都市左京区一乗寺門口町 27

Shobo-ji 正法寺
1102 Oharano-minamikasuga-cho, Nishikyo-ku, Kyoto 610-1153
〒610-1153 京都市西京区大原野南春日町 1102

Shosei-en 東本願寺 渉成園
Higashitamamizu-cho, Shimojuzuyacho-dori, Ainomachi Higashi-iru, Shimogyo-ku, Kyoto 600-8190
〒600-8190 京都市下京区下珠数屋町通間之町東入ル東玉水町

Shugaku-in Rikyu 修学院離宮
Shugakuin-yabusoe, Sakyo-ku, Kyoto 606-8052
〒606-8052 京都市左京区修学院藪添

Shuheki-en 三千院 聚碧園
540 Ohara-raikoin-cho, Sakyo-ku, Kyoto 601-1242
〒 601-1242 京都市左京区大原来迎院町 540

Tenju-an 南禅寺 天授庵
86-8 Nanzenji-fukuchi-cho, Sakyo-ku, Kyoto 606-8435
〒 606-8435 京都市左京区南禅寺福地町 86-8

Tenryu-ji 天龍寺
68 Saga-tenryuji-susukinobaba-cho, Ukyo-ku, Kyoto 616-8385
〒 616-8385 京都市右京区嵯峨天龍寺芒ノ馬場町 68

Tofuku-ji 東福寺
15-778 Honmachi, Higashiyama-ku, Kyoto 605-0981
〒 605-0981 京都市東山区本町 15-778

Yoshimine-dera 善峯寺
1372 Oharano-oshio-cho, Nishikyo-ku, Kyoto 610-1133
〒 610-1133 京都市西京区大原野小塩町 1372

Yusei-en 三千院 有清園
540 Ohara-raikoin-cho, Sakyo-ku, Kyoto 601-1242
〒 601-1242 京都市左京区大原来迎院町 540

Zenno-ji 泉涌寺 善能寺
34 Sennyuji-yamanouchi-cho, Higashiyama-ku, Kyoto 605-0977
〒 605-0977 京都市東山区泉涌寺山内町 34

Zuiho-in 大徳寺 瑞峯院
81 Murasakino-daitokuji-cho, Kita-ku, Kyoto 603-8231
〒 603-8231 京都市北区紫野大徳寺町 81

TOKYO

Chidorigafuchi 千鳥が淵
2 and 3 Bancho, Kudanminami, Chiyoda-ku, Tokyo 102-0074
〒 102-0074 千代田区九段南二丁目から三番町先

Dembo-in 浅草寺 伝法院
2-3-1 Asakusa, Taito-ku, Tokyo 111-0032
〒 111-0032 台東区浅草 2-3-1

Happo-en 八芳園
1-1-1 Shirokanedai, Minato-ku, Tokyo 108-0071
〒 108-0071 港区白金台 1-1-1

Joren-ji 浄蓮寺
5-28 Akatsuka, Itabashi-ku, Tokyo 175-0092
〒 175-0092 板橋区赤塚 5-28

Kiyosumi Teien 清澄庭園
3-3-9 Kiyosumi, Koto-ku, Tokyo 135-0024
〒 135-0024 江東区清澄 3-3-9

Koishikawa Koraku-en 小石川後楽園
1-6-6 Koraku, Bunkyo-ku, Tokyo 112-0004
〒 112-0004 文京区後楽 1-6-6

Kyu Furukawa Teien 旧古河庭園
1-27-39 Nishigahara, Kita-ku, Tokyo 114-0024
〒 114-0024 北区西ヶ原 1-27-39

Kyu Shiba Rikyu Onshi Teien 旧芝離宮恩賜庭園
1-4-1 Kaigan, Minato-ku, Tokyo 105-0022
〒 105-0022 港区海岸 1-4-1

Kyu Yasuda Teien 旧安田庭園
1-12-1 Yokozuna, Sumida-ku, Tokyo 130-0015
〒 130-0015 墨田区横網 1-12-1

Meiji Jingu 明治神宮
1-1 Kamizono-cho, Yoyogi, Shibuya-ku, Tokyo 151-0052
〒 151-0052 渋谷区代々木神園町 1-1

Rikugi-en 六義園
6-16-3 Honkomagome, Bunkyo-ku, Tokyo 113-0021
〒 113-0021 文京区本駒込 6-16-3

Shinjuku Gyoen 新宿御苑
11 Naito-machi, Shinjuku-ku, Tokyo 160-0014
〒 160-0014 新宿区内藤町 11

Shinobazu Pond 上野恩賜公園 不忍池
3 Ikenohata, Uenokoen, Taito-ku, Tokyo 110-0007
〒 110-0007 台東区上野公園・池之端 3

BEYOND

Adachi Museum of Art 足立美術館
320 Furukawa-cho, Yasugi-shi, Shimane 692-0064
〒 692-0064 島根県安来市古川町 320

Daichi-ji 大池寺
1168 Minakuchi-cho, Nasaka, Koga-shi, Shiga 528-0035
〒 528-0035 滋賀県甲賀市水口町名坂 1168

Isui-en 依水園
74 Suimon-cho, Nara-shi, Nara 630-8208
〒 630-8208 奈良県奈良市水門町 74

Kinchakuda 巾着田
125-2 Komahongo, Hidaka-shi, Saitama 350-1251
〒 350-1251 埼玉県日高市大字高麗本郷 125-2

Koraku-en, Okayama 岡山後楽園
1-5 Korakuen, Okayama-shi, Okayama 703-8257
〒 703-8257 岡山県岡山市後楽園 1-5

Meigetsu-in 明月院
189 Yamanouchi, Kamakura-shi, Kanagawa 247-0062
〒 247-0062 神奈川県鎌倉市山ノ内 189

Mori-shi Teien 毛利氏庭園
1-15-1 Tatara, Hofu-shi, Yamaguchi 747-0023
〒 747-0023 山口県防府市多々良 1-15-1

Ohori Koen 大濠公園
1-7 Ohorikoen, Chuo-ku, Fukuoka-shi, Fukuoka, 810-0051
〒 810-0051 福岡県福岡市中央区大濠公園 1-7

Raikyu-ji 頼久寺
18 Raikyuji-cho, Takahashi-shi, Okayama 716-0016
〒 716-0016 岡山県高梁市頼久寺町 18

Rinno-ji 輪王寺
2300 Sannai, Nikko-shi, Tochigi 321-1431
〒 321-1431 栃木県日光市山内 2300

Ritsurin Koen 栗林公園
1-20-16 Ritsurin-cho, Takamatsu-shi, Kagawa 760-0073
〒 760-0073 香川県高松市栗林町 1-20-16

Ryuge-ji 龍華寺
2085 Muramatsu, Shimizu-ku, Shizuoka-shi, Shizuoka 424-0926
〒 424-0926 静岡県静岡市清水区村松 2085

Suizen-ji 水前寺
8-1 Suizenjikoen, Kumamoto-shi, Kumamoto 862-0956
〒 862-0956 熊本県熊本市水前寺公園 8-1

Tsuki-no-Katsura-no-Niwa 月の桂の庭
Private garden, not open to the public.